THREE
NEW YORK
POETS

MARK AMEEN was born in Lowell, Massachusetts, in 1958. Twenty years later he followed an experimental theater company to New York City. He lives on the Lower East Side and continues to work occasionally as an actor. His first collection, *A Circle of Sirens*, was published in 1985 by SeaHorse Press. It is number one in 'The Trilogy of the Buried Body'.

CARL MORSE is the author of three books of poems, including *The Curse of the Future Fairy*, translator of a biography of Paul Verlaine (New York University Press) and the essays of André Maurois (Doubleday). Editor with several major publishers, he was for a number of years Director of Publications for The Museum of Modern Art. His lyrics and speeches for theater, written for Medicine Show Theater Ensemble, have been performed throughout the United States and Europe, including the Berlin and Bordeaux festivals. His articles and reviews have appeared in the *Village Voice*, the *New York Times Book Review*, the *New York Native*, etc. For the last few years he has presented Open Lines, NY – a series of readings by profeminists, lesbians and gay men from all over the United States.

CHARLES LAWRENCE ORTLEB Jr is founder, publisher and editor-in-chief of *Christopher Street* magazine and the *New York Native* newspaper.

G
A
Y

V
E
R
S
E

THREE
NEW YORK
POETS

poems by
Mark Ameen
Carl Morse
and
Charles Ortleb

Gay Verse from GMP, the Gay Men's Press
Series editor: Martin Humphries

Collection world copyright © 1987 GMP Publishers Ltd
Poems world copyright © 1987 Mark Ameen, Carl Morse,
   Charles Ortleb
This edition first published in May 1987 by
   GMP Publishers Ltd, PO Box 247, London N15 6RW, England
GMP books are distributed in the United States of America by
   Subterranean Company, PO Box 10233, Eugene, Oregon 97440

British Library Cataloguing in Publication Data

Ameen, Mark
   Three New York poets: poems by Mark Ameen,
   Charles Ortleb & Carl Morse
   1. American poetry — 20th century
   I. Title   II. Ortleb, Charles   III. Morse, Carl
   811'.54'08   PS613

   ISBN 0-85449-052-3

Photo of Mark Ameen by Becket Logan; of Carl Morse
by Susan Kuklin.

Printed and bound by the Guernsey Press Company Ltd, C.I.

INTRODUCTION

'I think every poem, and every figure of speech should be a matter of experience,' said Wilfred Owen whose poetry is filled with his own gay experience. So too are the poems in this collection of work by three outstanding poets who currently live and write in New York.

For many years almost the only openly gay poetry readily available in this country was imported from America. I used to regularly scour the shelves of Gay's The Word bookshop to see if any new (to me) chapbooks had arrived but it wasn't until i was editing the anthology *Not Love Alone* that i came into contact with the work of Carl Morse. I begin with Carl as he was the first poet chosen for this book and it was through him that i met Mark Ameen and was reacquainted with Charles Ortleb.

I was immediately attracted by Carl's funny yet deeply angry poems which are so informed by his experience of Gay Liberation:

> Sissy fairy/is liking librarians a lot/but finding
> clowns/just one more grim surprise,/like
> second cousins,/or the sudden fact of Eagle
> Scouts,/is never catching the eye of another
> sissy,/is chatting up the delivery man/for
> whom you have no past,/brushing his arm by
> accident,/praying he will go mad/and take
> your hand.

Besides Milton, Carl's biggest influence is his mother, a factory worker whose favourite saying (usually about the minister's wife) was 'She wouldn t say shit if she had a mouthful.' He has been called a cross between Corso and Firbank, described as a 'Devil with a crushed angel in his heart' and a giant fairy with one eye that never shuts. Carl particularly shares Harry Hay's determination 'that no young person among us need ever take [their] first step out into the dark alone and afraid again.'

In his work Carl specializes in the occurrence, at the same time, of the two variables: vulgarity and piss-elegance, thereby throwing into unsparing relief some of the ridiculous obscenities of the heterosexual culture. In some poems the anger displaces the humour as in 'The Curse of the Future Fairy' and 'Contra Naturam'. (From a British perspective, where a councillor was recently reported widely but not chastized for saying 'As a cure I would put 90 percent of the queers in the bloody gas chamber' [Cllr Brownhill, Tory Leader of South Staffordshire District Council] or Manchester Police Chief James Anderton is condoned by government leaders for promoting a moral crusade against us, such anger hardly seems misplaced.) What is unusual is that the anger is expressed so well in the form of poetry. Other poems articulate with wit and sensitivity the ways in which we experience the other world of heterosexuality that we are at once part of, party to and observers of.

It is the detail of experience that enriches the poetry of Mark Ameen. His first book, *A Circle of Sirens*, from which most of the poems here are extracted, arrived one morning in my post. I slipped it in my pocket to glance at on the tube (subway) and was captivated. In the same package were the sonnets, of which eight are included here, that form (along with *Monologue of a Dying Beast*) the second book in his 'Trilogy of the Buried Body'. The poetry is new, clear, provocative, funny, honest and streetwise. It is very direct. A songspeech which is demanding, unsparing and difficult to ignore:

Mark is my name. I try to work with
thoughts,/believing each to have a life all its
own./This is difficult, then, for in the stopping

6

of one/some others are missed, and one stares
into the space/from which they have just
exited upon lingering/teasingly for a light,/out
in front of your eyes,/where they'll blur when
the timing is right./The act of penning one
promotes immediate argument/along a
cohesive line,/or a structure sudden and blunt.

As poet Joan Larkin has said, 'the voice is filtered
through nothing but itself. It's as if I could see it, touch it: a
voice naked on a stage in a hot exposing light.' The *New
York Native* calls it 'a poetry which does not sublimate gay
life into metaphor, but exposes it':

But it is the idea of maintaining one's pride/
while suffering solitude after having known/
the love that provides the most tumult./
Everybody loves a happy ending./Oh, God,
what is this hunger?/At the heart of today
there is a heart./You just can't keep a good
race down.

'Militerotics' was the first Charles Ortleb poem i ever read,
it is a powerful political piece which presents the idea that
force and sexuality are intimately connected. I found
other poems in Felice Picano's anthology *A True Likeness*
which confirmed, for me, that he is a rare poet of
objectivity and detachment:

Today the scientists were suicidal./They found
a virus in heterosexuals/that they couldn't find
in homosexuals./They were sure that there
was some mistake./But no it was true./Disease
had begun withdrawing from homosexuals/in
protest of all the lies the scientists had told.

The poems here concern the effect AIDS has had on our lives, the politics of those in power, the family, life in New York, love and friendship. His precise use of language creates a poetry that sharply defines, bites, attacks and comments. He does not hold back from expressing the difficult realities of life, showing clearly how fragile the space we create for ourselves is, and yet how strong we can be if we wish:

> Listen to the phone calls they do not/make:
> 'Hello mommy, I hurt myself/erotically. Please
> come to New York Hospital.'/The doctors do
> what little they have time for, they're/all
> yuppied-out and tired of what/sin does to the
> bodies of other people/who don't own co-ops./
> We must learn to eroticize our wounds./The
> new love means getting it up/for things that
> are falling apart.

All three poets present a portrait of gay life today. Although geographically set in New York it could be the life experienced by any gay man in any urban setting. From the fragments of our lives these are both a record and a map of our changing world.

Martin Humphries

London, February 1987

Mark Ameen

Acknowledgements:
'They Make Watch Bands, Don't They?', 'Pass', 'Ink-A-Dink-A-Dink',
'It Is There', 'Two Excerpts from "The Mixed Report" ', 'The Radioacti-
vity of Radium', 'Very Well, Very Early, Very Well', 'Feelings Over
Miami', 'Projection Isn't Everything' are from *A Circle of Sirens* by Mark
Ameen published by Seahorse Press, New York 1985. The eight
sonnets are from a sequence of 22 appearing in *Those of You Who Are
Dying Are Very Gifted* by Mark Ameen. These two books form volumes 1
and 2 of 'The Trilogy of the Buried Body'.

It seems that Speidel is set to
put to market a line of bisexual watches.
Speidel, you remember, is the
maker of Twist-o-Flex.
Many the maiden Midwestern claims
the male line's too feminine for
any true-blooded beau, while
certain of the others wonder if
the women's are feminine enough.
Both lines, you see, look similar.
All watches, stylish, are said to
possess attractive straight bands
into which their faces disappear.
Those who respond are called respondents.
Those who don't are never called upon again
unless by some accident of timing
or a certainly unprofessional magnetism.
One respondent stated that his son would be
'worth every penny, and then some.'

And there's Jim-there,
On the roof
Where I left him,
Sunning his
Self.

I left him there, suspended in mid-life
Like a great dancer
Or a good firework
While I held my breath and counted
In the rooms below.

I left him there alone,
Then blocked around him
various scenarios of uncomplicated multiple orgasm,
the kind I witness being swept aside
on various anonymous streets of the mind.

I left him there and I turned green.

Ah, but there is no green;
There are but two colors to my cheeks:
flush and beet.

When he teased me
I blushed like Genet's Divine
Or an actor stronger than his director
who withstands humiliation through a profound need
Or an abused child smarter than his parents
who refuses to tell them to fuck off.

A child who has woven
the queerest of quilts –
A patchwork of constructs before activity –
and can honor his craft and history
only when alone
in rooms below,
spinning dark colors through into the stratosphere
with a flick of the wrist –

Until the rite is destroyed,
or maybe suspended,
by the sudden intrusion of
a hefty hairless arm wielding a broomstick
or brush designed for bruising.

I didn't mind.
Have you passed timeless moments when
the world snapped away because you
couldn't get a hard-on in a three-way?
I didn't mind.

Not when he recouped
by pulling me into a headlock
under a cafe awning
on an Upper East Side
designed for singles' fingernails and poodles'
    puffs,
and smashed one kiss against my mouth,
overturned my stomach and made the sidewalk
    disappear.

Not when he told me that he had sketched my neck
in his spare time.

Not when he says 'hi'
three or four hours
into a quiet evening.

Everybody is so lovely nowadays.

We are like two hard rubber bullets
straining against each other until sleep.
We do not shoot to kill.
We move forward directly to the point on the tongue
where the learned words held since Hollywood
still seek release –
we make ourselves vulnerable there –
and then we pull back –
teasingly and proudly
holding our suitor at bay
like Mighty Mouse lifting a white glove
to slow the path of a villainous pellet.
This is a pause, an assured moment,
and I am hung by what may be –
or suspended maybe.

I'll chew your beard to make you smile.
It was your hand I touched first.
We come together on
a fire escape welded stable by
messages delivered in absentia.
I haven't asked if you like roller coasters.

Man/Boy Love has become SOCIETY, INCORPORATED,
All in Caps, Please.
I mustn't argue, I am over twenty-one.

Classified Sex, Hard-Sell Illustrated,
or, The Biz Aspect,
hangs me up in an old closet,

Hangs me up by my jump rope,
your leg-irons strapped to my ankles,
grounding me at least.

So I sweat and think it over,
Gauging the heat.

The thermometer, suspended within
a phosphorescent cyclone of forced air,
there,
in your fish tank,
bounces with grace, a buoy,
maintaining vertical life.

The fishes, physical beasts,
cannot be seen. They hide behind the pet rocks
which make their homes aesthetically pleasing.

On the weekend
I can make your hand a harmonica
listening to the radio.

I can lie back and drink in
your animal body
as it putters in the kitchen.

Turn your face.

I see murder too.
Don't feel funny.
I have fucked you.

I see many people.
Expectant Guests,
not only as I nod into sleep.
Their faces are beautifully exotic,
sometimes conventional and tense.

All of them I seek, the Americans too,
but this morning I have fucked you.
Don't 'feel funny.'

The world ends as I walk out into it on Sunday.

You always leave in the morning,
Monday through Friday at least.

The dildo was flipping and flopping
because you told me it was in the closet
and now, I'm on the rug, jellied and flipping
    and flopping,
a fish under a kitchen table.
This is classified information,

But no matter how politely they ask,
I will not register for the draft.
Hush now, I'm working.

you know. There is a light.
It goes on no matter how I'm temporary and lost,
     so why?
We have worlds apart.
And I am seldom satisfied but in the night when
we bunch them together
under sacri-candlelight singing and peeing and
     slapping and drinking
and walk the block for Heineken, your hand poking
     spastically
my blue-jeaned ass.

This leaves me in a light in the morning,
a glow I don't need to demonstrate
but wish to stay home with in the absence of
     your soft
flickering
lengths.
This indeed is creativity.
New Age fecundity. A bright mystery in the
     Dark Age.
Retroduction.
I had days earlier walked the streets in your
     cock-ring, Levi 501's
and pink T-shirt feeling bound and dreaming of
     fresh dental floss
strapping my nipples as one more sinew
     connecting essentially all
movement to the body whole.
Oh if one might only believe all movement
     essential to the body whole.

If I might always feel as that became, the
   refraction of my physical self
to engage all passers-by with similarity, the
   deployment of my image
to everybody smiling in elasticity.
To be a chorus line within yourself.
Nothing extinguishes a jockstrap after it has
been pissed on.
Neither poetry nor music nor a stringent society.
I'm less and less enamored of seeking out a
singular acquaintance
when I've something else and you are not
   the answer.
Finding no feeling of belonging I say keep it.
One could spend a long life seeking a familiar
   feeling.
If there is a malevolence toward the world and a
   system of
individualistic placement, one had better use it.
There is still a sadness and I am seldom satisfied
   but in the dawn
of repeated birth, when discovering again after
   how many times
that there is something very important to be done.
Again and again there is freshness, brand new
   moments of
unfiltered life and sighing in need of free focus
   and a special care.
There is work and there is light.
Each dream is indeed a prophecy and the time of it
   is unfiltered.
Baby, baby, baby, baby take me away and tell me
   about
myself and we will
relax together.

Mark is my name. I try to work with thoughts,
believing each to have a life all its own.
This is difficult, then, for in the stopping
   of one
some others are missed, and one stares into
   the space
from which they have just exited upon lingering
teasingly for a light,
out in front of your eyes,
where they'll blur when the timing is right.
The act of penning one promotes immediate
   argument
along a cohesive line,
or a structure sudden and blunt.

I hear the rain out my window in the alley;
my window, too, it shakes.
Drinking coffee through the morning hours,
I push my legs through the sleeves of my bathrobe
and lie wrapped on the floor
wondering what my style is.
If I've something for everybody
who do I talk to when I'm lonely?
The moment, be it swept with indignation.
That the lube jar lies open beside the bed
because my man has decided that it would be nice
for me to beat off on him as he sleeps,
does this suggest that I'm not 'my own man'?
What would he do if I got fat?
'Still force you to love me.'
Just lucky, I guess.
What comes is what comes
and genuine becomes alien
when everybody believes the only vital stretch
to be the image of art and its usefulness.

Who needs a critical manifesto
when they can lube their way into a surefire
    notoriety?
It's not so bad, waiting on tables.
Try as you might, your deepest dish is a thematic
    line.
How does one rid oneself of a structural
    reputation?
Music.
A jury.
The medicine is collecting my amoebas.

We mustn't forget that 'the good things' and
    many another
entity inevitably in quotation make us feel
    quite well
inside. For instance, a clean apartment and
    somebody
to talk to. Another feeling arises of having
    bought a
pair of boots. But mostly one feels unworthy of the
social animal stigmata.
There's no earthly reason to present people with
    scag.

Freshness again...devotion to things at hand.
A cigarette, burning from its light, suspended,
on the groove of a glass ashtray. Moons and moons
    and moons...
Too much description may indeed get us no place.
I desire voices anew, a receptive anxiety
to which they might be attracted.
One needn't be constantly on top of things.
In a glance one gets the joy of catching up.
A young Clark Gable staring from a red brick wall
tells one a lot about writing and the ways
we lay hold to passages for glimpsing
the very latitude of being a human being
committed to the planet Earth.

To think that the world has already exploded into
a great shower of meteorites
is a fun thing as I lie.
My tits ache splendidly, pin-curled.
It is difficult to know things and yet to remain
    decorative.
Knowing to say enough is enough is probably a
    good thing
but I will probably not ever know it well enough,
like the sinewy man in the fantasy hotel,
whose body made me long for a bedroom without
    walls,
who, seeing my quivering commitment,
agreed to let me shut the door,
and who says, without crossed intentions,
'That was beautiful but it could go on forever.'
I could transcend the foreplay
if you extend the latitude.
What do I really want?
Talking with a friend I am inhabited of a lofty
    spirit
along the spine who signals me to be large long
    and knowing
then looks out through my eyes as a great artist.
Each of us has our moments,
and then there is a touch of nausea.
Yet crawling into bed seems a home of sorts
    at least.
One needs to do things in front of people.
In a gorgeous line of resonant sameness the poet
    says something.

* * * * *

Saturday comes and we are to dance.
An unfamiliar club. The best kind.
We entered left.
One man sat at the running board getting
    a blowjob.
The young man sucking lifted his head to kiss
    the cock-man's
face and was swiftly pushed down.
An unpleasantly collected physique strutted in
    jock-strap
and black Oxfords.
I sensed this was not a dance bar.
Jules pretended not to.
I turned around watching myself as a young man
    sprawled
across the bar shirtless to be whipped by the
    bartender.
Jules was put off, as if this sort of thing were
strictly American. I was wretched momentarily
    though
a good part of me wanted to hang out. By then
and especially later.
We went upstairs.
Jules dances in small, periodically frozen spasms,
living snapshots directed towards separate
    fragments
of the crowd. We performed in a circle of light
under the sway of a thick accent. He says that
'dancing is a part of the sex,'
so I give way and agree for the time being.
Masculine muscularity and effeminate tendency
coalesce into a concern for clothes. He dressed
twice on the way out, and showed me his shirts.
At points inside postures he would focus my way
only long enough to say, 'Are you going to go
    to bed with me?'

In that playfully introverted way much as after
    sex he said,
'It was good, yes?' and hours later from apparently
    anywhere,
'Shit, I really dance crazy, don't I?'
He's so aware of what his surface is doing
that he can't think of anything to say
and he never seems to be where he is.
For sex he ties a cord around his cock
and I feel my anatomy shifting.
Jules is very nice in one direction.
On Sunday Jim and I met and took alternate cars
    on the BMT.
In the morning I worry.
I think that some of us may be initiating a
    belief system
which escapes so many of the others for whom it
    has become
all numbers. Or maybe that's just business.
Still, I may be healthy only when I am alone,
and suppose that one must get tough in many
    fashions
so as to preserve the antithesis in other arenas.
Too many are overachievers in unconsciousness.

Mr T. says that he always remains friendly
with boyfriends after splitting
and when I mention that I've not yet been able to
he says, 'Well, I hate to bring in age,' (this is
    in the morning)
'but I am thirty-seven and, quite possibly,
as one gets older it's not just sex and when
the physical dies there's still something
to hold on to.'
So I tell him that complete splits were not my idea
in either of the two instances, were and are in fact
a strain, and that Harry is thirty-four and Jim
    forty-two.
'Well, then, I take it back,' says Mr T.

Very Well, Very Early, Very Well

He brought me champagne, for a housewarming,
and fruit, for our bodies,
and we caught ourselves a 'buzz'
and made love with our voices then we fucked.
At three-thirty in the morning we woke and
walked with me on crutches to a neon eatery
where he bought me breakfast and a hot
    fudge sundae.
On the street he kissed me goodbye for the
    first time.
Let me say that I enjoyed the walk home.

(I'm feeling hot and grounded.)
Unless I'm playing myself again,
this could be the start of something big.
A Grand Plié over Mt. St. Helen's,
spiked with an adjustable mound.
In the way of spices
we kiss the day goodbye,
trollops under the sway of
Mocha Java mixed with Tip O' the Andes
and chewed into availability
by a neat machine which whirs and sputters the
    action.
Two blades, simple and curvaceous,
are set to blossom.
The red dot is pressed and they disappear.
This is done in a flurry,
and apparently animated,
but they don't do anything
unless the lid is on and there is no danger.
Eeek.
Now, what about brunch?
One member per guest.

I decided to examine myself and cannot get over
how much paper I needed.
This had been going on for some time.
The tossings of my daily trysts are
collecting themselves upon the carpet.
Some people are afraid to throw anything away.
Not to mention finish anything. In that horror
as to where you will be left hanging.
Emptied of that which to look toward
with repulsion and not a small dose of
sick love. Cleaning the house, halting
an assault or being done with this.
Oh, I pray only to be abhorred in a vacuum
and to spout forth in full flavor into
Everybody's Onanistic Livelihood,
the one tenacity they have conditioned themselves
to develop in for they have commissioned themselves
not to talk about it.
Coitus interruptus was thrust upon us
the other evening and we decided not
to say anything about it, but boy did
I have a party when somebody finally
brought me home.

There was the thought that a somebody
might come over and get me and when
he does you'd better watch out.
Better not cry.
Speaking of the pause between the thought
and what to do with the telephone wherein
one doubts the very necessity.
Some such a cord, either a woman or
a celebrity, and that the fool is no
longer in trouble.
'It wasn't blood it was motor oil.'

Apart from muscle we've a long way to go.
As to the great love affair of my past
(and it *is* accumulating, my dears),
'I tried to make it into a masterpiece and
any great creator will tell you that a work
is never completed but at some point surely
abandoned.'
It was an absurdist endeavour, sort of like
trying to decode transgressions while
suspended between the poetry and the park bench.
In the annual log of the Caligula Market Research
    Company
a perfectionist is said to have been 'sissified
    and abstruse.'
See recondite.
Sort of like that man, so very beautiful,
whose wall was finally broken down by the
rip in your pants ('such a neat idea, I don't know
where you find the time to carry on so perfectly')
and then while talking you discovered a major
    part of
his vocal life to be so disgusting that you were
vastly relieved to see an old friend whom you also
hadn't liked upon meeting. Now these, assuredly,
are testimonials to be cherished in that they
transcend the love of brawn, don't you agree?
Why, yes, of course it makes me feel good.
Why, sure, yes! I love the attention but I am
no snob I guarantee you. I met a most beautiful
man at the very tip of that iceberg weekend,
went away with him and made beautiful love.
I had to eat a full pint of chocolate on the
    way home
in order to remain on the ground.
Sometimes, upon rising, it takes courage to
do anything else. And so we leave it at that
and invent a scenario for extricating ourselves.

The two boys at the bar were beautiful and
    intelligent
and I will leave them there until they realize it.
Leaving the movies one realizes the import
of doing so.
But it is the idea of maintaining one's pride
while suffering solitude after having known
true love that provides the most tumult.
Everybody loves a happy ending.
Oh, God, what is this hunger?
At the heart of today there is a heart.
You just can't keep a good race down.

1

'Constantly risking absurdity'[1] here
Where I rhyme my way out of history
Nonetheless murders literary fear
And affirms all present-tense mystery.
I don't want to flash only personas,
Especially not on the glaring page,
Nor merely to pick sexual boners –
I want properly to sing of my age.
My age is in struggle for attitude
As it defends itself against a past
Where no group is given real latitude
But each one is kickier than the last.

Well, it's true, I may lose face in the mist
But I'll find something tighter than a fist.

1. L. Ferlinghetti

2

The circus is not the only place
To swing above the heads of your audience.
Ask me, I know a very lonely place
Which provides a singular ambience;
Which achieves its arrival by leaving
Young men in suits dripping Crisco and tweed
Hanging on the street. Look at me, grieving
Again, when I had every chance to succeed.
God, let this be the end of poetry
Or at least a tardy start of my youth.
'Wasted on the young,' says the dominant he,
But *my* youth has been wasted on the truth.

Alone here, I'm dripping A's, B's and C's,
Sick again, the 'Am I alive?' disease.

8

Tony Sweet, surrogate seraph of love,
Surreptitiously abandoned my cause.
Majestic limb lamenting the Above
Gives semioticians occasion for pause:
Your gesture – natural, Greek and ironic,
And limned of proper cynicism –
Is fueled by a current which, while tonic,
Implies theatre for effeminism.
Actor in discontinuous motion,
You discard one pose to freeze another;
Strong-arm pathos a seductive potion
But you speak all the while of your mother.

You called me pussy, I felt like a wife.
And then you retreated, spared me my life.

Terrence, let you be my man from Philly;
Lord knows you did your growin' on the farm.
Baskets packed in leather make me silly –
Chain-man, I wear your glow: it's my alarm.
I'll cook you breakfast next time, you just sit
And read my fuck-poems with some orange juice
And dry toast – Oh, babe, you be a tight fit,
You scroungy bastard, you hot bloody moose.
I'm not sure what's coming down over me;
My body red neon, my head torch blue –
I come from women most men never see
And with them share a bridge and tunnel view.

Filler like that, I can't remember when.
Oh, babe, hot man, I'll never shit again.

You're white trash in the best sense of the word,
My smelly little rock'n'roll swinger.
Set on the crash course of a broken bird
Whose home nest couldn't nurture a singer.
The garbage and gophers of St Mark's Place
Offer me a pigment of something real,
As your flat, all draped in lavender lace,
At double your small income is a steal.
Your security is in your swivel
And the way your frozen locks ring your neck.
You're lucky, they still transcend the drivel
Of your cool stance, your nasty kid's dreck.

Pretty boy, I was hoping you weren't numb yet,
But when the phone rings you ask, 'Did you
   come yet?'

More than life's eyes, here in your home,
Is the aura of leather and longing.
The crack in the plaster houses a gnome
Whose more than life-size phallus is gonging:
'Dick...dick...dick,' and as I slip my mind through
Into your epaulets and march on out
The door, I am easily made blind to
Intelligence, which knows the morning pout
Following even the hottest meeting,
The emergency of self without crust
Or costume, the spread-eagle, red, bleating
Romance, the diamond cutting deeper than lust.

Oh, my darling, I am slight, pretty, and slick
When in your tanned hides I'm ticking
   'Dick...dick...dick.'

21

On a very hot Independence Day
This elongated Manhattan summer,
The boy of hard darkness, the mad sashay,
Decides that life is no longer a bummer.
While his sweat pours down on Avenue B
And his heart can be claimed by no other,
He says, 'Oh, young self, do you not yet see?
You've a calling, you're every man's brother.'
And so you must wait and attend to life,
Exposing brick and greeting thy neighbor.
No need to spend thought on this living's strife –
The world itself does you the favor.

It's a time when personal panic fades:
This is the very first summer of AIDS.

22

I don't think I believe in 'gay life'
Although I know how to dance in a crowd.
But when the coroner inserts his hot knife
I think they will discover I was proud.
I don't think that I believe in 'straight life'
Although I was a junkie with the rest.
In my intestine they'll recover my wife,
Whom forever has put me to the test.
I have thought that I believe in 'my life'
But the credo is tenuous at most.
I think I believe only in 'high life'
And in my life I've tried to play the host.

Anyway, Death gets all the attention
In this womb we're not allowed to mention.

Carl Morse

Sissy Fairy
The Curse of the Future Fairy
Dearly Departed
Unbecoming Friends
Rives Gauches
Frenchie
Inmates
Contra Naturam
Stagecoach
Digital
Elegy for Ruth (1930-1954)
Term Papers: Humanities I
                Humanities II
Summer Stock
Kinderscenen
Wanigan
Night Drive
Toward Evening

Acknowledgements:
Some of the poems by Carl Morse have appeared in the following
magazines: 'Sissy Fairy' in *Christopher Street* Vol. 7, 4; 'Stagecoach' in
Bay Windows, Boston, July 1985; 'Inmates' in *The James White Review*,
Spring 1986; 'Contra Naturam' in *The James White Review*, Spring
1987; 'Night Drive' in *Kennebec*, April 1979; 'Digital' in *Seditious
Delicious 2*, Spring 1984; 'Term Papers' in *Shenandoah*, Vol. XXXV, 4.
Other poems by Carl Morse appear in *Not Love Alone: a modern gay
anthology*, GMP 1985.

is saying the wrong first words,
not hitting back, astonished,
liking strangers more than your parents,
wishing your brother and his friends would die,
getting out of the house at dawn
and visiting the road,
asking little girls if you can play,
not hitting back, astonished,
trusting bugs,
spotting vicious aunts and uncles
and tying them up in dreams,
thinking about getting to school safe,
planning how to get through recess,
planning how to get through lunch period,
planning how to get through phys-ed,
planning how to let Superman know,
giving the paperdolls gorgeous evening gowns,
giving the teddy-bears serious operations,
helping the sugar ants dig holes,
giving them sugar,
naming the hens,
not pulling the skin off trees.

Sissy fairy
is liking librarians a lot
but finding clowns
just one more grim surprise,
like second cousins,
or the sudden fact
of Eagle Scouts,
is never catching the eye
of another sissy,
is chatting up the delivery man
for whom you have no past,
brushing his arm by accident,
praying he will go mad
and take your hand.

Sissy fairy
is sneaking *Muscleworld* and *Family Circle*
while secretly training to lead parades,
hanging inside with the women
who talk people and food and clothes,
not hanging outside with the men
who talk cars and guns and cunt,
is watching wallflowers
and wanting to punish God.

Sissy fairy is trying to see
if holding your head
like Audrey Hepburn will do any good
since nobody seems to want to hit her,
at least for long,
and everyone feels so extra glad
when she is finally glad.

The unborn fairies are angry,
and the interplanetary anthill future is saying
step up the search for lifedust in new galaxies,
for the ground is no longer here, the air
   not here,
not here the sweethearts of the satellites.
And the 20th century is dead,
and the 21st century is dead,
and the 22nd century is dead,
and the 23rd century is full of fairies!

For all the commands to alter and delete did not
   print out,
and they have survived to colonize the bowels of
   sissy pulsars,
flaky formations of frisky zygotic giant heartbeat
   fairies,
zipping about on errands of interstellar pervert
   mercy,
nursed in the secret victory gardens
of Provincetown and World War III.
And the baby fairy of the silly fifty states
giggles itself to pieces in its crib.

So if there be any 23rd-century-minded fairies here,
turn to your neighbor either side and say:
'A survivor fairy loves you.'
Indeed, let us be reverential for a bit
and listen for a rustle in the room,
for the rustle of our unborn fairies.

*

But for those who glaze their fairies,
who tie and gag their fairies
in the bassinets and taxis of the Lord,
in choirlofts and classrooms,
and MacDonald's bathrooms,
whose greatest creation is Astroturf
and a doll with nothing between its legs that shoots
    at fairies,
I say *deathdust*.

And for those who paint their fairies pink and blue,
who inject their fairies with Cheerios lie serum,
who cauterize the orifices of their singing fairies,
who stun and rape their kissing fairies in
    bucketseats and Barcaloungers while splashing
    together in the golden shower of primetime
    powerpiss,
I say *deathdust*.

For the unending supply of uniform-part-men
    lined up for powerplug while sucking on nerve
    bombs and invading the biospheres of future
    fairies unto the last quasar,
I say *deathdust*.

Deathdust as you attempt to leave.
Deathdust before you reach the door.

You others, however many, kiss now,
and be glad, and go lay wreaths
on the tomb of the Unknown Fairy.

When caught between his smelly mounds,
I totaled 67 pounds.
Dropping his primed and hairy frame,
it is a game,
he said, and fun.
I kept looking directly at the sun.

Quickly I learned to stroke his head
and get myself carried home and fed.
He weighed 200, stripped and felled,
and when he came, he yelled
and yelled and yelled.

Today, according to the news,
we are no longer sharing views.
Husband and father, sorely missed,
not a bare spot left unkissed.

And now I can fix my face
and wash my dolls in peace.

I start telling you again the crazy kind
of turn-on Dale is and how doubtless
he'll be famous with such breakdowns
in the three loose-hole texts done by seventeen
and it's then all right now he should die tomorrow.
And you start giving me the we-love-you-André-Gide
-but-what-is-this-shit-about-little-Arab-boys
    treatment
and another slip of veal.

If instead he of course were she,
like honey-blonde,
with the lithe curved legs of class,
you'd decide you were getting in on the starter
    floor to heaven
with the latest Sylvia Plath,
yielding to each imagined fuck or blow,
and didn't I deserve her love.

Rives Gauches

(for Helene Zahler, for Louise Mally)

Yours is the spinal marrow served
with the broth of the weaker sex reduced:
'How a merciful God kept the white man hard,'
'Had Bismarck but heeded nature's call,'
and 'Mrs Kropotkin and oral clout,'
laced with your dread of romance and of being right.

Magazines slide to the rug,
new outposts of printed life for the cats,
as we spread our vigorous limbs and tea
among the samizdat.

These little pigs go to market,
like a bus on the sidewalk
haunting the democratic way.

'Just what would we know about men?' you snap.
'By then certain girls will have got to be pissed.'

Frenchie

We've decided to make a wonderful couple,
me and ce chie-en-lit poilu,[1]
his menhirs eloquent as kissed pensées,
serving up bacon slides between unshaved apple balls
and woodsmoke armpits for Cartesian afternoons.

Speaking of trapper Bob, Ignace
can stitch a hem and pulp,
as well as snowshoe, sugar off,
and exhibit the kind of paddle trick
that becomes the beaver[2] trade.

Call me Madame de Pollux Staël,
a voyageur on either breast
as inmates from another teepee browse my femurs
and I lose control of the canoe.

Mojicri![3] Must transportation be the matter
after all these English years?

1. hairy shit-a-bed.
2. [Fr.] castor.
3. [P.Q.] Mon Jésus-Christ.

Inmates

Since Bruno asks for me
and cell doors slam
I sleep with his big toe in my mouth.

Mornings I lick his bowl and spoon
and lie down in his shaving stubble
and listen to the news.

Sometimes I tie his loafers to my breasts
and masturbate with his driving glove
and go out all refreshed.

Evenings I hold his nuts
as he sniffs the wash
and we watch TV.

I love his alumni file,
his dog act,
and the unobtrusive service.

In rooms with such appointments
surely the traverse rods will work,
and the guards line up to watch the stars
and slide their sacred pouches
up and down the bars.

'[Homosexuality is] ordered towards an intrinsic moral evil, and thus the inclination itself must be seen as an objective disorder...[it] may seriously threaten the lives and well-being of a large number of people...when civil legislation is introduced to protect behavior to which no one has any conceivable right, [people should not be surprised when] irrational and violent reactions increase.'

– Letter to the Bishops personally approved by
Pope John Paul and issued (October 1986) by
the Sacred Congregation for the Doctrine of
the Faith (once called the Inquisition).

'[Homosexuality] is an error of degenerate individualism that is contrary to nature...All homosexuals are cowards; they lie just like Jesuits...If we don't encourage this correct heterosexual behaviour, we will have sexually disturbed youngsters, not the right material for the elite SS, the new Holy Order...the Poles present a special problem...We must exterminate these people root and branch...'

– from the writings of Heinrich Himmler,
including Directives from his Department for
Combating Abortion and Homosexuality
(Berlin Gestapo Headquarters).

'And with the guts of the last priest, let us strangle the last king.'
                                              – Diderot.

Contra Naturam

John Paul arranges his skirts around the throne
and releases his jaws and bowels,
and the sacred light comes shining forth,
and twenty more fairies die.

One is thrown off a bridge in Maine.
One is cornholed under the rainbow with a
    cut-glass crucifix.
One's lifetime services are no longer required.
One decides not to bother to call the nurse.
One says good-bye at school. She is fifteen.
One orders another stinger.
One catches the edge of the underpass.

Fairies make you forget yourself at scrimmage.
They polish and warm the saddles of your Mopeds.
They live in Big Macs.
They smear themselves with mousse and Brie.
They drink the blood of spaniels,
and they try to touch your hood.

When the celebrant cried Kill a Queer for Christ
the congregation climaxed
as the turned-on networks moaned and flashed
insertions of the Popemobile
and broke out reruns of The Robe.

John eats his peas with a silver fork.
His curtains are nicer than yours or mine.
His fly is edged with the lace of blinded dykes.
His wet dreams come in pouches.
If the sheets abrade his stainless thighs,
the world of finance licks its fur.
His waste valves seize as tightly as
the sphincters of atomic plants according to their
    annual reports.

The pick-up trucks stream back from their retreats,
their roof-racks floppy with the frames
of fresh-clubbed egg-and-butter fags.

If you sit on a baby fairy, Jesus smiles.
If you make a big one beg or bleed,
your spirit dines in paradise
on pickled pervert dink and tongue.
If you off an entire pill-box, then the Virgin
drops her chopper on your lawn
and takes you up to heaven in her lap
and lets you suck her cunt in front of God.

Stagecoach

Hardly a sweetheart has survived
the masked man in the old corral,
yet somebody's god is at home in Butte,
and the ancient tribes are disposed like ants
in the shade on the forest floor,
mandibles in working shape,
immune to the spat about space.

The West was once a greener place,
if you care for giant ferns,
and then it became what we know today.

Once in the dark the movie train
backed up for me and Sally when we chased it down
   the track,
but the film turned out to be Humoresque
where the heroine's arms give way to the sea
and the art of the violin.

Tolerating the motion of the carriage is another art.
'Mais vous m'avez fait descendre mes bagages,
   Monsieur!'
'Excuse me, but the only Americans we knew
were worse than the Germans.'

A clean sweep of the valley
where some of the deputies take the time
to spruce up the bunkhouse
as well as develop
the cut of the herd
might do a posse a world of good.
Carl has agreed to check out the bars
and report if the symptoms of lust and its theory
apply to this afternoon's saloon.
But then there's the danger of meeting Melville on
    the pier.

Perhaps after all it would be ideal
just to rest here among the Chinese baskets
and the flats for the summer show.

'Now the defining of our sentiments has long been a preoccupation of religions and of governments. And the most powerful of these tie-ups has always been music's marriage to poetry.'

– Virgil Thompson.

Digital

Now that the sound of the life of sound is
      inspissated to its inert private parts
to be doled out in just-add-eau-and-fist-me-
      till-I-lose-my-marbles-master cookies
by the traffic officer who will also catalog
   your fillings,
Mozart is the latest centrefold.
All that vigorous pumping.
All that reinforcement of the status quo of
   poignant loss,
the violins like baby veal marsala,
with Flute a randy prelate's porn
and Coronation Mass a picnic at the Pentagon
with prairie oyster drums.

Köchel was a little mayor of New York.

Nobody knows the key signatures I've seen
– certainly not Pablo Casals, who, clitoris by
   clitoris,
      is defusing the revolution,
– not John Cage whose unlubricated interfemoralisms
      doth make fugitives of us all,
– not Zubin Ozawa Bernstein whipping the Mahler
   bottoms up
      as cooled-out trustees beat off on their Prontos
      behind the banks of one-way mirrors,

– and not Beverly Sills, whose operas are
    inconceivable
            without the domestic tiff, good breeding,
            and the personalities of the inventors
                of acid rain.

Elegy For Ruth (1930-1954)

Depending on the shingle style, the house seems
   dark,
though conversation flickers on the porch
like 'Why do the poles attract each other?'
         'How should I know?'
         'Don't get upset.'
and a number of expressions still beat film,
such as 'riddled with cancer,'
preceded by 'They say she was,'
that knot of distant aunts,
and 'When they opened her up,'
which is nearly another entire unit of interest,
like a codfish waiting to be baked in milk,
and barely celluloid,
or so I thought, remembering her crewcut
and the merriment of 'Kitten on the Keys.'

Thus we await dessert,
embarrassed by the shudder of the maid.

'You smell great,' I tell you,
pressing your knees in fun.
Indeed, other statues in the park are claiming
   speech,
and today several lovely points of view flew up
when I stooped to retrieve my bag.

'He do the police in different voices.'
    – Dickens, *Our Mutual Friend.*

Term Papers   *(for seven voices)*

Humanities I

Excuse me, but the teacher has come to pass.
This time she had drunk real deep,
and we laid her out on a giant sponge,
one more apparent victim of the assignment with
    no name.
When next a freshman pulls a knife,
yell 'Unannounced quiz!' and hug him hard,
moaning 'kiss, kiss, kiss, kiss, kiss, kiss, kiss'
until the potential vote hugs back or fights to get
    away or dies.
First find your seat, then circle the flight desired.
How did it happen?
Can't tell yet.
If you like, we can spend all recess skipping rope,
or seeing guard dogs actual size, or language arts.
FREE DOROTHY.
How do you play house?
Don't know
I do. Put vaseline on the doorknobs to keep out the
    kids.
'People who live first-hand lives
are the exception rather than the rule.'[1]
FREE MARY AND MARTHA.
Is it your house or theirs?
No, your house.
What's its name?
Alhambra?
I don't think so.

Finished or not, pass all books to the front.
'Où les nervures de la voûte aboutissent-elles?'[2]
Vacations Bruce and I play harvester in bed,
forging the link of Thanatos to Eros
and the rise of class.
Who feeds you?
Pizza fairy.
With tickles?
Yeth. What are you doing now?
Writing it down in the secret book.
I hear soldiers on the roof.
No, rain.
No, soldiers. Maybe cows. And pith.
Sunday I memorized Le Cid
and then saw The Women to learn how to keep
    my man as an elective.
'We are going to be happy.' (Ruskin)
EAT THE RICH.[3]
Christmas?
Not now.
SURRENDER ELEANOR.
Try to stay with your group.
LOOSE JOINTS.
'My horse is white, and a white horse is not a horse.'[4]
Is it home yet?
Hush.
Fridays I hide the welcome notes downstairs
and bone up for finals in chemistry with Bill.
No talking before the bell.
Soldiers for sure?
For sure.

1. Charlotte Wolff, *Bisexuality: A Study.*
2. *Holt, French I.*
3. bumper sticker.
4. Kung-sun Lung, fl. 294-259.

The boy stood on the flooded porch
mouthing the dialogue for help
until a noble uomo waded out
and threw him on his shoulders like a sack.
'Ma dov'è il duomo?' murmured I
into his thatchèd vertebrae.
'Tre dollari,' he grunted, heading south.
Oh Dennis, are these but the souvenirs
of yet ein and're translucent maid
reading inscriptions in the vestibule?
I'll do anything oval.
You mean oral.
You're not Italian.
Ici est tombé a narrative heart
thc flamcs did not attain.
Oh Leo, are these the tergiversations merely
of encore un autre pissed-off polyphile
proposing famished gods?
'The theater becomes a habit. Life does not'
  (Nijinsky).
Rabbits are habits, but nuns are something else.
Some days I feel like Hildegarde
or a new expression on the blackboard,
even as this loaf
was previously scattered on the mountains.
What are you doing?
Shaking you.
Why?
Because you like it.

Oh Tom, this had better not be ancora un altro
evident tragedy wreathed in joy
('At the edge of the porch, you may get a green
    feeling caused by a nearby bush')[1]
or yet another nest of surd occlusives
whence it takes 'forever' to bewray
that a big fairy pudding is not the same
as a pudding for big fairies,
however laced with visions of
e.g. Il Duce crooning Stardust at the Paramount.
'Then all of a sudden the Pilgrims had a big
    surprise.'[2]
ARBEIT MACHT FREI –
and faking love is also liberation
in states where sight-lines kill.
You're making it up.
I ith not.
Rats.
NEXT CASTLE, PLEASE.
Oh Ludwig.
Croth my legs and hope to die.

1. Tony van Hasselt, *Outdoor Watercolour Workshop.*
2. *Holt Social Studies, Grade Three.*

The outlook is good for curtain calls
if you are possibly Pekinese,
but let's never rehearse these premises again.

Screening took off with the child in the wings
yelling Have a Nice Day and Go Bye-bye
while trying not to lose its spot
and the crude effect of the juvenile lead
on the plot for a permanent cast.

Meanwhile we polish a limited run
of the ever-astonishing smash walk-on
of two bad boys being good
while juggling a shitload of postcubist procedures,
rethreading the Popeye reel,
and setting class lights.

Remain calm in an emergency
and I'll show you the speaking part for love
– which is what most of the stagehands say
right after they come in your jewel song.

Some people brought their own scripts to the
    chautauqua,
not to be gulled by wampum or applause,
one tied spread-eagled to the wind-whipped flag,
howling for a bellyful of god,
another faking exit cues.

So we policed the litter around the bandstand,
including the Pampers,
and left the Expo momentarily a better place.

Trace the history of poetic diction. Five pages.
'Distraught over the divorce, he shot the jaw off
    Walter Leigh, a graduate of Westbrook High.'
'My business is parking lots.'
'For six hot inches, call Feliz.'

Actually we got through previews best
on a smattering of yachtclub Greek and train
    Italian.
'Thalassa. Thalassa! Pericoloso sporgerse.'
And once: 'Treib' andern Schmerz.'

But at last the secret was Chester Arthur,
and across the board we broke all house records
wadding the program into balls
– with rarely the sense of too many perfect
    pitches in the room,
as when Sally picked up her lines and walked
and the butler sighed like St Sebastian
at the end of a long hard play.

Kinderscenen

(for my sister)

The fairies are taken into the world
the way children are taken from women,
their fears taken from the limbs of their brothers,
their flight taken from the roofs of their fathers,
their sight taken from the breasts of their mothers,
their hopes taken from the eyes of their sisters,
and they eat their own placentas.

No, we can't share all the kisses and slaps
of the modern screen
– but the shade, yes,
window, yes, and the rain
– and a cold glass of life
handed down from the sink;
also the secret doors of food,
the alarm of being dressed for snow,
the boot that stays tied all day,
the introduction to the bus.

What's so odd about letting me near your kids?

Yet we often agreed
on privacy,
cheerleading,
fashion,
the stars,
and no one left out of the Valentine box;
also to comfort our rained-on dolls,
pretending their faces were still O.K.

We share the teatowel over the bread,
the crumbs under the rack,
the uneven slice;
we share the serrated edge.

By a glance during study hall let you know
when your skirt was good
and please not to care
when the shape of your lipstick spelled despair
wishing you could see him nude
and trying to shave
himself   himself   himself

We are the women the Men invent
when they can't get it up for your easy ass.
You are burning my jack-off porn
for the good of the middle class.

Night after night I set out to undress
the men I walked home on the silver screen,
and one by one I tried to compress
his own big love between my legs,
like marriage in a mezzanine.

Ever watch a fag hit a dance floor high?
                    break a three-way tie?
                    be the funny guy?
Ever watch a dyke look a stud in the eye?
We know how to make short visits work.

As the silent dates arrive for you,
the obedient fairies brush their teeth
and improve their nails
and work on their phoney scrapbooks.
They don't have to be punished to make them lie,
and they beg to be fucked when scared to die.

As the rescued princess begins to sweep,
the fairies are watching the woods for the witch,
at the gate,
on the back of the stove,
by the crib,
in the unmown grass as you ride by,
also standing in line,
crying over a book,
and planning their own escape.

Wanigan

(Abnaki) *a trap – that into which something strays*

And so we disburse such idia of adaptive
   strategy as:
Just how oviparous do you plan on getting?
I want my tail back,
and Do you really eat it skin and all?

Some rat says:
Even a large snake not in the mood to feed
can be killed by a mouse.

Less cartilage and more matter, please.

The yellow woman picks up the charred baby
she insists on dressing like a boy
although its legs break off
like drumsticks at the knee.

Here then as elsewhere strayed among
the radicands of love,
I can still tell who's being related to,
especially on those vacation days
I imagine the tent to have animal acts
and the woods to be lined
with an excited multitude.

You haven't lived until you've run over a cat.
The last thing you see are the eyes.
the last thing you hear is the thud
near the bulge of the universal joint.
There's no point ever in going back
except with a torch and gun
in case it should still be twitching
– for who wants to be clawed by a dying blur
or get tough with a tire jack?

Remember: it could have been a horse.
Remember: it could have been Billy or Martha
                 Graham.
Remember: life can be uneventful.
Remember: it had a mouse in its mouth.
Remember: it was Patroklos whom we truly and
                 dearly loved.

Having accounted for another outing
of the good child strapped in the stroller
trying not to cry or pick its face,
the famished angels on the roof,
and cleanup of the gelatinous goosh
called the hind end of the dead cat
under the refrigerator,
the election of late afternoon retreat
is now extended to
the corner of the gazebo where
tea is a monument,
earth wears its condom,
and (as the painting turns toward conversation)
John is Agnes Tiepolo,
Jimmy, Larry and Jane Pissarro,
me Winslow Rauschenberg,
and nobody Rosa Oldenberg
because no sentence has yet to get an
   ironing-board's ass too big to walk around
   down right.
Meanwhile, the patient staphylococci
huddle on the bread-knife,
hoping, like Barbie, staring at Ken's raised arm,
getting picked up will mean a new career,
and babies and a decent home.

Charles Ortleb

Beginning
The Truth About AIDS
Double Trouble
Paper Plates
A Poem in the Tradition of Jasper Johns
Epiphany: 249,330
Unity
Sex Change
The Answers
An Army of Tricks
Prisoner X
The Party
Metaphor as Illness
Ending
The Moody One
Opacities
4 A.M.
My Mother Chewed Ice
Another House of Being
Family Therapy
[Untitled]
Haunted Fresco
On Finding Out That The One You Slept With The Night
    Before Was Murdered The Next Day
This New York

Beginning

My writing always rises like circus
   tents, for circuses that
   never open
but I'm always prepping, putting up
   posters in new towns, boasting of
    new beginnings
   everything I am is
in some way a bright beginning.
How can I die if I consist of
   so much beginning?

Today the scientists were suicidal.
They found a virus in heterosexuals
that they could not find in homosexuals.
They were sure that there was some mistake.
But no it was true.
Disease had begun withdrawing from homosexuals
in protest of all the lies the scientists had told.
And in the laboratory of Dr Essex,
the most amazing thing had begun to happen.
The vials of homosexual blood, in neat little racks
with lavender labels, had begun to rumble.
The blood in the tubes had begun to boil.
The vials had become so hot
that not one of the Havard experts on homosexual
viruses could handle the tubes without
suffering third degree burns
on their Nobel prizewinning research hands.

Dr Essex began calling round, and yes it was true
in every laboratory at the Havard school of
Public Health, the blood in the test tubes labeled
homosexual had begun to boil.
And a red steam began to rise throughout the
Harvard School of Public Health, a hot red steam
from the vials of blood labeled homosexual.
And all of the scientists, all of Dr Essex's
    assistants,
and even Dr Essex, began to gasp and cough as they
breathed in the hot red steam from the
boiling vials of blood labeled homosexual.

And all of the scientists fell over,
gasping through the red steam for some of the clean
cold collegiate air of Boston, began to hemorrhage
from the very mouths from which they talked
to each other all those years,
around those test tubes with the homosexual blood
about the homosexual problem.
And their lungs, as they gave out their final air,
had turned into red hot balloons
filled with red homosexual steam
from the vials of boiling blood labeled homosexual.

Double Trouble

When the schizophrenic
develops Alzheimer's disease,
he forgets
all the wonderful
people he was.

When the Alzheimer's patient
develops nymphomania,
the love that he makes is
the most pure, the most innocent.

When the kleptomaniac
develops pyromania
he always burns down
the things he loves.

Paper Plates

When the epidemic
first hit,
Pelly and his boyfriend
were invited to
a family picnic.

They were having a wonderful
time when all of a sudden
they looked up and
noticed that the rest
of the family was eating
their meal on
the family china, and
that the two of them
were eating theirs
on paper plates.

Suddenly they didn't
feel well,
they couldn't swallow.

A Poem in the Tradition of Jasper Johns

Think of something you
are afraid of. Then add to it
an additional thing you
are afraid of. It is now time
to add three things you
are terrified of. Add
something you are horrified
about. Now we have it.
The setting for the day
he left me.
The setting for the day
all the lovers
rip out a piece of the world
and add
the dreaded
additional thing
we are all
afraid of.

I saw an odd dog outside the
bank yesterday, white
with pink eyes and then I saw its
owner, a misshapen woman standing
there studying her money and then
looking up at the sky
and then the dog looked up
and then she looked down
and their eyes met and
they married, and I realized they were safe.
They lived in a world without men.

Unity

This is why we are all
one person, if we seized
any one of you, and
stripped your
clothes off you
and went through your
pockets, we would find a
small piece of paper
on which would be scribbled
our universal code:
toilet paper, trash bags,
catfood, and juice.
And don't forget the onions.

Sex Change

There is a woman
trapped in my body
who will not go to
Denmark for the operation.
She refuses to leave Manhattan.
Previously, the woman trapped in my body
has been pregnant three times
and we've aborted.

But now the woman trapped inside my
body is pregnant again,
we've decided to have the child.
We think it's a boy
trapped inside the woman
trapped inside my body.

Someone asks again:
'But if we all have AIDS,
Why were the gays the
first to die?' I answer:
'Because they
were the first to be murdered.'
Someone tells me that
they think the
government
is prolonging the epidemic
till all the gays are dead,
and I say, 'They'd better
not prolong it
till all the gays
rise from the dead.'

An Army of Tricks

(for M.D.)

An Army of Tricks
doesn't lose any major
battle, it withers in the
barracks on
the embarrassed
unlucky nights when the hour of
hair was misparted
or the Archangel of Bad Sex
picked out one who
left the toilet seat up,
one who sang Carol Channing
in the leather sling.

An Army of Tricks
too drug-intravenous
for battle, too ravenous-romantic
to establish a heartland,
an Army of Tricks, design-polite
and infirmary-bound,
will delight the bachelor-nurses and
the viral, breakthrough doctors
and make easy the
overweight nights of the coupled enemy.

Prisoner X

The first thing the prisoner did was
remove his clothing
in deference to his date with a system.

He knew he had no rights,
so he gave up his clothes.

He handed them to the guards and asked that they
shoot him first.

Knowing full well that after you are nude
there are further undressings:
fingernails, genitals, fingertips.

You are nude as a howl.
When you are nude the guards
are your father and mother.

When you are nude, death and love are in charge.
They reach for your things.

The Party

People arrive by novel and poem
at this party of words
and they leave by
reputation.
I have talked in party to authors.
I have talked in author to parties.
The quiches of genius are passed from
king to queen to prince of metaphor
to duke to duchess to knave of
irony to serf to maid to
slave of fame.

Listen to the phone calls they do not
make: 'Hello mommy, I hurt myself
erotically. Please come to New York Hospital.'
The doctors do what little they have time for, they're
all yuppied-out and tired of what
sin does to the bodies of other people
who don't own co-ops.
We must learn to eroticize our wounds.
The new love means getting it up
for things that are falling apart.

Ending

When I lose someone I become a kitchen person.
From potholder to napkin
the plot gets thin.
It is not complex to be without you.

People in doorways
are just lovers in doorways.
Lovers in doorways
are just people in doorways.
I've been one and the other.
You've had me both ways.

In one broken bed
where romantic lovers
furiously invented each other,
nothing is getting even
And it is loud.

You leave.
It's over.
The divine connection
of our differences is over.
We both go back
to being a lot
like each other.

In a circle of friends there is one   who seems

to be in charge   of the innerness.

Over a period of   great friendship,

while the others   talk and externalize,

they trust that   one moody soul

to be full of   bottomless thoughts,

and over a long period   of ambiguous friendship,

it becomes clearer and clearer   that even

the tiniest thing the inner one   contributes to

the group   is actually the

ground, the pithy light, the monogamous center.

At love's center there lies
a wicked forgetfulness, love is
never all nostalgia.
Love envelopes the mind
in darkness, and navigates for night.

And in the darkness of loss,
the other darkness at the door
when he moves on into another love,
you recall that even when things
were sweeter than air
it was dark and you were dark.

And if I could go from lover to
lover once again, in a few hours,
touching all of them, fetching
each one again for but a few warm seconds,
you would hear about a dark man
who made opacity out of his opacities
and some would say 'what he did for love'
and others could vouch for the darkness.

4 A.M.

I am learning
that when he doesn't
come home he is
having a good time
and yes that is
unfaithful, but the earth so
desperately needs good times,
unfaithfulness, and water.

My Mother Chewed Ice

Man's relationship with ice
begins in the womb
while his mother is
drinking her whiskey sours
biting, breaking, bashing the cubes
warning the balls of men
sending microchips of the world's ice
into the
birth of his soul.

In his room with his thought-things
his lover brings him a meal
to eat with his food for thought
and mail to place beside
his unmailed thoughts

It is a house where one man thinks
the other man dances where they
want each other to be and at night
they trade nakedness
putting on nude versions of each other
they form man among the dance shoes and the
    thought-things.
And for a while
there is no orgasm
that is not another
house of being
where all is welcome.

Family Therapy

I love   your little trips
back to your   family. You
leave, looking   like a friend
who is a perfect   lover
and you return   from your momma
and your poppa   a sick wreck.
You have undergone   that form
of cobalt family therapy   called
                nuclear familiation.

[Untitled]

What were you fighting about?

I don't know.

Where?

Our apartment.

And now?

Two separate souls in the street.

Who are you terrified of now?

My lover.

And who before that?

My parents.

And before that?

The wet bloody dark.

What do you love?

Men and furniture.

What loves you?

Furniture.

If one horror should
see another horror
in the nude,
If one horror wears
only a towel
and is greased up
and wants a fist
up its anxiety,
If I find suspicion
clinging to the
racks, waiting for its
Saturday night beating
by contempt,
If I find innocence
waiting in the steam room
for experience, If I find
self-consciousness
playing all night
with the candy machine
and haughtiness
pacing around the whirlpool
with loneliness
and greed
finger-fucking poverty
and intelligence
sucking off
stupidity
and hysteria smoking
a fast cigarette
with patience and comity,
and creation,
bleeding and stoned
trying, while tied to a bed,
to come one more time,
then I know
I'm at the baths.

On Finding Out That The One You Slept With
  The Night Before Was Murdered The Next Day

I got his name and phone
number
but then the name
appeared in the *Times* the
next day as a body.

True, that's all he
had been the night
before, and true, both
I and the murderer
had entered him, one
by a hole that was there,
and one by a hole that
had to be made.

And maybe both I and
the murderer, as we
entered his body, were
both equidistant from
the core of his love.

or maybe there really
was no quarry of
love there at all,
no rock of love, no
ballast or bullshit, just
the perfect trick,
a convenient victim.

Or he must have felt
something. Either I or
the murderer must
have moved him a
little before the police
moved him.

I like to imagine
his childhood – his
mother processing his
nakedness and how
from the first strange
spoonful of his babyfood
and from the chill of his
first anal thermometer
you just never know
how many people are
going to get in.

How many dirty glasses does it take
to make one New York?
How many smokey trains?
How much of a coating of urine on footprints
does one fun city require?
How many bloodshot, reckless eyes
looking through the dying trash
dining on the smoke and the urine
and filling the footprints
does God want in this New York?
How many talk shows does He want
us to talk back to?
How many answering machines does
God want to leave messages on that are never
returned in this New York?
How many sparrows does he keep
outside the windows of doomed lovers
just to keep His eye on this New York?
I have faith that New York is the
only sparrow that He really cares about.
How many of our ecstasies packed
into agonies does it take to make
this sparrow, this New York?

Gay Verse from GMP, the Gay Men's Press

SO LONG DESIRED
Poems by
James Kirkup & John McRae
ISBN 0-85449-038-8
64 pp   UK £2.95/US $5.95

DREAMS AND SPECULATIONS
Poems by
Paul Binding & John Horder
ISBN 0-85449-039-6
64 pp   UK £2.95/US $5.95

TONGUES UNTIED
Poems by
Dirg Aaab-Richards, Craig G. Harris,
Essex Hemphill, Isaac Jackson &
Assotto Saint
ISBN 0-85449-053-1
to be published Autumn 1987

NOT LOVE ALONE
Martin Humphries (ed.)
Anthology of gay verse
by 30 modern gay poets
ISBN 0-85449-000-0
144pp   UK £3.50/US $6.50